Jean Conil's
Slim Cook Book

Vegetable Dishes

These calorie-rated recipes show how to slim on a wholesome, nutritious and exciting meatless diet. Included are recipes for breakfasts, snacks, main meals, salads and refreshing drinks, plus a suggested seven day menu.

Cover picture shows Stuffed Peppers with Peas and Soya
(see page 32)

Jean Conil's
Slim Cook Books

Vegetarian Dishes

Easy-to-prepare calorie rated recipes
based on the New Style Cookery

by

MASTER CHEF JEAN CONIL

and

DAPHNE MacCARTHY

THORSONS PUBLISHERS LIMITED
Wellingborough, Northamptonshire

First published 1980

ISBN 0 7225 0539 6

Photoset by Specialised Offset Services Ltd., Liverpool and printed and bound in Great Britain by Weatherby Woolnough, Wellingborough Northamptonshire

Contents

PUBLISHER'S NOTE

The authors are not believers in 'crash' courses, and they recommend a planned approach to slimming over a three to six month period with the emphasis on a balanced diet and regular exercise.

The calorie ratings given in the recipes which follow are almost entirely for the raw ingredients. They should be regarded as approximate only since it is impossible to allow for the inevitable differences between one portion and another of the same food, especially in the case of meat which contains hidden fat.

Introduction

Over-weight can be caused by bodily imbalances but, usually, it is the tell-tale sign of over-eating. What your body does not require immediately it stores as fat that has to be carried around wherever you go. The best thing to do is to get rid of it; not in a sudden massive starvation campaign but gently and easily, by cutting down on fattening foods, keeping a check on what you eat and being sensible. However, anyone who has a big weight problem should consult a doctor before starting on any slimming diet as there are those who do require medical supervision.

In this book there are vegetarian recipes for breakfasts, snacks, main meals, desserts, salads and refreshing drinks. Some include milk, cheese and eggs while others avoid all dairy products as well as eggs. There are recipes, too, for making soya and nutty milks and home-made bean curd.

Every recipe ingredient is calorie-counted and so is every serving portion. This enables readers to keep a check on how many calories they are consuming; makes it possible to substitute ingredients (as long as the total is amended) and shows how to create your own dishes along similar lines.

Apart from the recipes there are suggestions on varying the dishes, and also handy cooking hints.

We both firmly believe in using as much fresh fruit and vegetables as possible in the daily diet and recommend the consumption of at least one salad a day. We also believe in getting value for money when shopping, and we have given some shopping tips.

At the back of the book we suggest menus for seven

days, four based on 1,000 calories and three on 1,500 and all providing the opportunity to have a little 'extra' of your own choosing each day.

Vegetarian Dishes

The International Vegetarian Society describes a vegetarian as someone 'who abstains from flesh, fish and fowl'. But vegetarians can further be divided into those who include dairy products and eggs in their diet and those who reject such foods. Like everyone else vegetarians, no matter how strict they are in their beliefs, must have a well ordered diet to stay healthy, which means they need a daily intake of protein, vitamins, mineral salts and all the other necessary nutrients. Where non-vegetarians get much of their protein from meat and fish, vegetarians must opt for other things. There are plenty of suitable alternatives.

Nuts provide protein. Unfortunately they tend to be high in calories which precludes a wide use of them in a slimming regimen. Even so, some recipes in this book include nuts in moderate quantity as well as peanut butter because of their food value.

Cheese is another excellent source of protein. Again there is the snag that many cheeses have a high calorie content. Nevertheless, as it is a firm favourite with many vegetarians, we have used a little in a number of our recipes; making more, though, of cottage and curd cheeses which have less calories than the hard kinds such as Cheddar and Cheshire.

Eggs are also useful for their protein. They are cheap, keep well (if stored pointed end downwards in a cool place) and are versatile in the kitchen. Furthermore they do not tot up a high calorie total. As these are barred by strict vegetarians they too have been used sparingly.

Dried Beans, Peas and Lentils

It is the pulses, the dried beans, peas and lentils, which are acceptable to all vegetarians and which play an important part in providing protein in the diet, that have been made much of. These dried foods have been essential for centuries to people in lands where meat is hard to come by. They are inexpensive, keep well in airtight containers, and can be used in all kinds of recipes. They do, though, need to be soaked before being cooked and are best when they are reasonably fresh. They should never be cooked too quickly. Some have to be soaked for several hours, over-night if possible, others, especially if they are fresh, need a shorter soaking time. There are two schools of thought about this soaking process. Some people prefer to put the vegetables in a bowl and cover with cold water and leave; others put them in a saucepan, cover with water, bring to the boil, top with a lid, remove from the heat and leave. Either way the soaked vegetables have to be drained after soaking and cooked in fresh water.

There are different opinions as to when salt should be added to the pot; either at the beginning, in the middle or right at the end of cooking time. Try each way for yourself to test which you prefer. It pays to cook more dried vegetables than are needed for one meal. The left-overs, drained and cooled will keep in a refrigerator for up to four days and are ready for use in salads, fillings or for reheating.

If you want to cook a smallish quantity in a trouble free manner put them in a pot with plenty of water, bring to the boil, cover and simmer for ten to fifteen minutes, then transfer the vegetables and water to a wide-necked vacuum jar. Check there really is a lot of water and room for the beans to swell, then seal the jar and leave for six hours or so. The only way dried vegetables can be cooked really quickly is in a pressure cooker, but, no matter how they are cooked, any that have been in store for months will need a longer time to soften than fresh samples.

Among pulses are dried peas, which can be either whole or split; lentils, either red or brown; kidney beans; butter beans, haricot beans; black beans and chick peas.

Not all are particularly light on calories but a little of them goes a long way!

Soya Beans

From a food point of view the soya bean must be the most important bean of all. Soya is considered to be the food of the future because it is so rich in protein and other essential nutrients. It is available in various forms, some of which, like dried vegetables, need to be soaked. The soya bean can be eaten when small and green; as bean sprouts; ground to a powder, or as texturized soya in chunks, strips or mince. Many of the commercial brands of texturized soya have additional vitamins to provide even more nourishment. These chunks or strips usually need to be soaked to hydrate them. Instructions are given on the packets but we also mention our methods in the recipe section.

An alternative to cow's or goat's milk is made from soya and a bean curd (recipes for both are in the book). Soya milk can be purchased from health shops and bean curd – tofu – from certain Oriental stores. The Chinese describe tofu as 'meat without bone'. Soya flour is a good source of nutrients, a concentrated food in the same way as dried egg powder. The flour can be used in many kinds of recipes including cakes, bread and the enrichment of purées. These pulses not only contain protein but other essentials as well. Dried beans, for example, provide iron, potassium B group vitamins and vegetable fibre.

Sprouted Seeds

Vegetarians can grow some of their own foodstuffs simply, cheaply and efficiently in the smallest of areas. No garden is required, just a little space in a room or cupboard, a few empty jars plus the necessary seeds. Well planned 'gardening' can reap a regular harvest of fresh produce that contains protein and vitamins, can be used in salads, savoury dishes and as a delicious additive to cakes, bread and biscuits. Among possible crops are Alfalfa, Mung beans (bean sprouts), Fenugreek and sprouting cereals. Nothing is grown beyond the sprouting stage.

Probably the best known of them all are the bean sprouts which can be bought ready grown in some supermarkets. These sprouts have a very high food value and are particularly good for their vitamin E content. Although they are comparatively new to the West they have been used in Eastern cooking for a very long time. Bean sprouts are crisp and crunchy. Alfalfa contains at least 40% protein, is high in vitamin content and has a delicate taste to it rather like that of a very young garden pea. Fenugreek has a spicy flavour. It is good for its iron and vitamin A and is particularly tasty in salads. Sprouting oat cereal has a tempting nutty taste; the other cereals in sprouting form are malty.

You can grow these bean and cereal 'seeds' in almost any kind of container but really ideal are clean empty coffee jars with holes punctured in the screwtype lids. This is because there must be full access for air as well as facilities for easy drainage. Mung beans have to be grown in a dark place (the sprouts develop a bitter taste if left in the light), other kinds of seeds can be kept uncovered as long as they are away from direct sunlight. None should ever be grown in a draughty spot. Place a smallish tablespoonful of seeds in the base of a jar, less with Alfalfa which must have a lot of growing space, then cover to about five times the depth of the seeds in warm water, put the lid on and leave to soak for several hours. Drain by turning the jar on its side. Rinse well with warm water twice a day, three or four times a day for soya beans, to keep them moist, but drain off the water after each rinsing. This is necessary because if left in a pool of liquid the seeds may rot. Some 80-100 hours after germination the vitamin content of the sprouting seedlings are at their highest, and they have plenty of flavour. Cut the sprouts when about two-inches (5cm) in length and, for maximum food value, eat them raw. Any not immediately needed can be stored in a refrigerator for four to six days. The sprouts can be steamed; added to casseroles, curries, soups; quickly fried, tossed in salads, or chopped small and used in cake, biscuit or bread recipes.

As we have stated cereals can be used for sprouting at

home but cereals can also be widely used in other ways as well. The main kinds are rye, wheat, millet, buckwheat, pot barley, oats and rice. All are inexpensive ways of getting vitamins and protein. They cook quite quickly, particularly millet and buckwheat, both of which can be simmered in ten to fifteen minutes. Cereal bran is a very good source of dietary fibre.

Further Suggestions

Much has been written over recent years about the need for roughage in the diet. The inclusion of bran is one way of guaranteeing it is there. Other ways of ensuring fibre in the daily foods is to eat a suitable breakfast cereal, have fruit with the skin on, consume nuts, salads, pulses and brown rice. Among low calorie foods recommended for their fibre are Brussels sprouts, cabbage, runner beans, broad beans, bran, watercress, tomatoes and raspberries, but anyone suffering from colonic disorders should seek medical advice as to what they ought to eat.

Wholemeal pasta is something that vegetarians should use in their catering; this is a wholesome food and easy to prepare. Having tried it once, the chances are you will thereafter prefer it to the 'white' pasta. Use wholemeal flour rather than white flour in your cooking, occasionally, with a mixture of one or more of the following: coconut flour, soya flour, corn meal, rice flour and ground rice. We also recommend you get the unpolished brown rice rather than any other, but try wild rice sometimes, too.

Wild rice is really the seeds from a type of wild grass and is delicious. It was the staple food of the Sioux and Chippewa Indians and is making something of a 'comeback', although it is not all that easy to find. Keep it in a tightly covered container in a cool dry place and it will last indefinitely. There is a recipe using wild rice in this book; it is ideal for savoury dishes and for special occasion entertaining.

For those who may be worried about not getting sufficient protein or vitamin B in their food wheat germ is an excellent additive, but remember it is approximately 100 calories an ounce (25g) when adding up your calories. Buy it little and often as the fresher it is the better. One delicious way to enjoy wheat germ is to spoon some into a carton of yogurt, sweeten with honey and have for breakfast or a snack meal.

Milk Products and Substitutes

Both of us are very much in favour of yogurt although we do appreciate there are those who, because of their food beliefs, cannot have it. Natural yogurt is a delight in the kitchen as it can be used for instant sauces, dressings and desserts by simply adding the flavouring or sweetening of your choice. Yogurt can be used in cooking, is easy to digest and is a sound basic food. Incidentally yogurt diluted with milk or tomato juice makes a refreshing drink.

Milk is a basic food, too, but even those who accept milk in their diet should restrict their intake when slimming. There are skimmed milk powders as well as bottles of skimmed milk available which are lower in calories than full-cream milk and are very good. For those who do not want milk from cows or goats there is the already mentioned alternative of soya milk. There are others that can be made from nuts, one recipe for which is in the recipe section of this book.

The curtailment of milk for drinks does not mean that cups of tea are no longer possible. Ordinary tea served with a slice of lemon is refreshing, so is lemon 'tea', made by pouring very hot water over a slice of lemon. This when sweetened with honey is heartening as a breakfast drink. There are plenty of herb teas to make. These are brewed like tea and can be served with or without milk, lemon or sweetening. Tastes vary as to how strong herb teas should be. To begin with, try adding three teaspoonsful of chopped fresh, or one teaspoonful of dried, herb per pint of boiling water. Brew, covered, for five to ten minutes, strain and serve, then if a stronger, or weaker, infusion is preferred the quantities can be changed next time. Many vegetarians don't drink coffee. However, decaffinated or dandelion coffees may be more acceptable and are certainly worth trying. Cocoa is fattening, so if a chocolate-type drink is wanted buy a carob-based beverage from your local health shop. Carob beans are something like cocoa in flavour, much lower in calories and can be purchased in powder form. For those who fancy a piece of chocolate now and again, particularly those prone to migraine attacks, we suggest they buy confectionery made with carob.

Nibblers' Temptation

Of course slimmers should not often cheat by eating confectionery. They should avoid sugar as much as possible and, in any case, there is plenty of natural sugar contained in many foods, especially in fresh fruit. Honey is a good sweetener but don't be heavy-handed with it. One ounce (25g) totals 82 calories. It is handy though when you are tired as honey is a speedy provider of energy because it contains large proportions of the simple sugars levulose and dextrose which require very little digesting and are quickly absorbed into the blood stream.

One of the most testing times when trying to lose weight is if you feel peckish or are, by habit, a nibbler and cannot resist temptation. If genuinely hungry (which you should not be with our recipes) eat vegetable sticks, fresh fruit or a little dried fruit. Fresh fruits are very reasonable on calories and can be had the year round. Buy for value. For instance, when getting pears, unless they are to be consumed immediately, do not choose ripe samples. Buy when still hard, and allow them to ripen off at home. You will know when they are ready because a mature pear will yield to gentle pressure at the stalk end. Ripe pears quickly go past their best and are then only suitable for cooking.

Raw Fruit and Vegetables

Soft fruits to be eaten raw should be just ripe, fresh, clean and firm with the punnets unstained at the base. Really ripe fruit can be pulped for speedy sauces or cooked.

Never pay top prices for cooking plums, only pay this for first quality dessert samples. For maximum flavour select ripe eating apples but don't ignore any small ones, which are often cheaper and packed full of sweetness and juice.

Raw fruit and raw vegetables are always important in the diet; you do not have to spend money on fuel to cook them so be prepared to spend just a little extra in getting the best. This is vital when buying green vegetables which need to be firm, crisp and really fresh. An excellent guide is that if a cabbage, for instance, looks good enough to eat raw then it will be. Winter kinds of greens adapt very well in salads but, in either hot or cold weather, it is better to prepare salads shortly before they are to be served, unless they need to be marinaded for flavours to blend, in which case they should be covered and stored in a cold place.

While practically every vegetable can be eaten uncooked, some of the root crops such as potatoes are usually served cooked whether to be eaten hot or cold. Try not to over-cook them, though, or 'drown' them in too much water and, perhaps most important of all, remember to keep the liquid in which these vegetables were cooked to use as a stock.

It is widely appreciated that fruit juices make refreshing drinks; so do vegetable juices and mixtures of fruit and vegetable juices which can also be used in cooking. Sometimes a little vinegar is added to give a little variety; for this and for salad dressings we suggest cider vinegar which contains malic acid. Malt, wine and distilled vinegars contain acetic acid. Cider vinegar has been recommended in folk medicine over the ages for rheumatism and for slimming.

Breakfasts

STRICT

MENU 1

(two portions)

	Calories
Nutty Milk Compote	**695**

Calories per portion: 348

To drink:

1 cup lemon verbena tea   —
or
1 cup dandelion coffee   —

NUTTY MILK COMPOTE

$\frac{1}{2}$ pint (275ml) Nutty milk (recipe below)
$\frac{1}{4}$ lb (100g) Apples, sliced
2 oz (50g) Plums, sliced
1 Orange, peeled and segmented
2 oz (50g) Walnuts, halved or chopped
1 oz (25g) Sultanas

Mix fruit with the nuts, divide into two individual bowls
and serve with the nutty milk.

NUTTY MILK

	Calories
2 oz (50g) Skinned almonds	340
2 oz (50g) Desiccated coconut	356
1 oz (25g) Soya flour	120
1 oz (25g) Honey	82
Pinch of salt	–
2 pints (1¼ litres) Water	–
	898

Calories per pint: 450

Combine all the ingredients in a saucepan. Simmer gently to boiling point. Leave to cool. Liquidize.

N.B. This milk is good to serve with cereals, muesli, porridge and so on.

MENU 2

(two portions)

	Calories
Porridge Bee	**506**

Calories per portion: 253

To drink:

1 cup verbena tea	–
or	
1 cup dandelion coffee	–

PORRIDGE BEE

¼ lb (100g) Quick porridge oats
½ pint (275ml) Water
Pinch salt
1 teaspoonful (5ml) Honey
1 teaspoonful (¼oz/5g) Wheat germ

Bring water to the boil, sprinkle in the oats, cook five
minutes, add salt and remove from heat. Stir in the
honey. Serve with the wheat germ sprinkled over. Eat on
its own or with nutty soya or skimmed milk. (If having
milk add more calories).

MENU 3

(one portion)

	Calories
¼ pint (150ml) Orange juice	60
2 Nutty Bites	approx 156
	—
	216

To drink:

1 cup mint tea	—
or	
1 cup dandelion coffee	—

NUTTY BITES

(makes 8 bites)

2 oz (50g) Soya flour
1 oz (25g) Wholemeal flour
½ pint (275ml) Nutty milk
Pinch salt
1 teaspoonful (5ml) Baking powder
½ tablespoonful (8ml) Oil for frying fritters

Thoroughly mix salt, baking powder and the flours together. Mix in sufficient milk to make a batter. Very lightly oil a small thick-based frying pan, preferably non-stick). Cook 8 x 4 inch (10cm) fritters. Serve piping hot. Unused fritters can be frozen for another occasion. (Total calories for fritter mixture is 627).

Variation:
Although these fritters are delicious eaten on their own they can be served with honey, fresh or stewed fruits.

MENU 4

(one portion)

	Calories
¼ Small ripe melon	approx 8
2 Corn Cakes	approx 172
2 teaspoonsful (10ml) Honey	50
	—
	230

To drink:

1 cup camomile tea	—
or	
1 cup dandelion coffee	—

CORN CAKES

(yields ten approx)

2 oz (50g) Corn meal
2 oz (50g) Wholemeal flour
1 oz (25g) White flour
Pinch salt
1½ teaspoonsful (7.5ml) Baking powder
Approx ½ pint (275ml) Nutty milk
1 tablespoonful (15ml) oil

Thoroughly mix the flours, cornmeal, salt and baking powder together. Add sufficient milk to make a firm batter of dropping consistency. Oil a large thick-based frying pan or griddle and put over a low to medium heat. When hot drop batter from a large spoon onto the griddle, cook gently until firm and brown on the underside, turn and cook the other side. Serve immediately with honey. Unused corn cakes can be frozen for later use. (Total calories for corn cake mixture 858).

WITH MILK AND EGGS

MENU 1

(one portion)

	Calories
½ Grapefruit	15
2 Wholemeal Pancakes	approx 93
2½ fl oz (65ml) Blackcurrant yogurt	63
2 teaspoonsful (10ml) Honey	50
	—
	221

Serve pancakes with the yogurt and honey.

To drink:

1 cup lemon tea	2
or	
1 cup black coffee	2

WHOLEMEAL PANCAKES

(yields sixteen-eighteen small pancakes)

¼ pint (150ml) Skimmed milk
2 Eggs, beaten
3 oz (75g) Wholemeal flour
1 oz (25g) White flour
Water
Pinch each of salt and baking powder
1 tablespoonful (15ml) Oil for frying

Sieve salt, baking powder and white flour together. Mix
with the wholemeal flour. Combine milk and eggs
together, beat into the flour with sufficient water to make
a smooth pancake batter. Cook the pancakes in a small
pan, no more than 6 inch (15cm) diameter. The pancakes
can be stacked on a plate over hot water while being
cooked, or they can be laid out separately and when cold
wrapped and frozen for later use. (Total calories for
pancake mixture 742).

MENU 2

(two portions)

	Calories
½ pint (275ml) Apple juice	100
2 slices Sesame Spread	474
	——
	574

Calories per portion: 287

To drink:

1 cup lemon tea	2
or	
1 cup black coffee	2

SESAME SPREAD

2 x 1 oz (25g) slices Rye bread
¼ lb (100g) Cold mashed potato
2 oz (50g) Tahina (sesame seed paste)

Make sure the potatoes are free from lumps then mix in
with the tahina. Pile on bread slices and cook under hot
grill for two to three minutes. (Tahina is available in cans
from Greek, Oriental and health shops.)

Variation:
The Sesame spread can be laid over wholemeal toast if
preferred. Peanut butter can be used instead.

MENU 3

(four portions)

	Calories
1 pint (550ml) Buttermilk	200
Bean Croquettes	1,147
	1,347

Calories per portion: 337

To drink:

1 cup lemon tea	2
or	
1 cup black coffee	2

BEAN CROQUETTES

1 x 5 oz (150g) can Baked beans in tomato sauce
3 oz (75g) Hazelnuts, chopped
1 Egg, beaten
2 oz (50g) Wholemeal breadcrumbs
Salt and pepper
1 oz (25g) Soya flour
1 tablespoonful (15ml) Oil (for greasing tray)

Drain sauce from beans and reserve. Mash beans well. Combine with nuts, crumbs, seasoning, then bind with the egg and a little of the reserved sauce if necessary. Divide into croquettes, dust with soya flour and arrange on a lightly oiled baking tray. Cook in oven at 400°F/200°C (Gas Mark 6) for 15-20 minutes. Serve hot or cold, accompanied by the heated sauce diluted with a little water or milk.

Main Dishes

STRICT

CHICK PEA AND VEGETABLE CASSEROLE

(six portions)

	Calories
½ lb (225g) Chick peas, soaked overnight	640
7¾ oz (220g) can Baked beans in tomato sauce	213
1 lb (450g) Onions, chopped	80
Salt and pepper	–
1 fl oz (25ml) Oil	260
2 oz (50g) Walnuts, coarsely chopped	310
Bouquet garni	–
Sprig fresh mint	–
	1,503

Calories per portion: 250

Place soaked chick peas in a large fireproof casserole and cover with four to five times their volume in water. Bring to boil on top of the stove, removing scum as it rises. When broth is clear add more water to replace that taken off with the scum and by evaporation. Add mint and bouquet garni. Cover and transfer to oven preheated to 350°F/180°C (Gas Mark 4). Cook for 2½ hours. Replenish pot with more water when necessary to keep the level constant. Leave beans to cool in the liquid, (this helps the peas to soften more thoroughly). When cold, gently reheat sufficiently to liquify the stock, strain. Remove bouquet garni and mint leaves. Reserve the liquid and the chick peas separately. Heat oil and shallow fry the onions until tender but not browned (with a little stock to prevent burning), add chick peas and beans, stir and blend in the reserved tomato sauce. Season. Add walnuts and a little more of the chick pea stock. Serve piping hot.

Chef's tips:
(1) Use remainder of reserved chick pea stock for soups.
(2) The long process of soaking the dried peas (or any similar dried vegetable) and then slow baking makes the most of their food value. However, if cooked in a pressure cooker soaked chick peas take thirty minutes to cook.
(3) For something different make the above recipe then liquidize or sieve to make a purée. Flavour with lemon juice or crushed garlic and serve cold as a dip.
(4) Chick peas are known in some shops as garbanzos. They can be purchased ready-cooked in cans.

SPINACH AND SOYA PIE

(four portions)

	Calories
7 lb (3kg) Fresh spinach	560
½ lb (225g) Onions, sliced	40
1½ fl oz (40ml) Oil	390
½ lb (225g) Swedes, sliced	40
¼ lb (100g) Texturized soya mince	200
½ pint (275ml) Hot water to hydrate the mince	–
1 tablespoonful (15ml) Soy sauce	7
1 oz (25g) Wheat germ	100
2 teaspoonsful (10ml) Marmite or yeast extract, diluted in 2 tablespoonsful (30ml) hot water	12
2 oz (50g) Walnuts, chopped	310
1 lb (450g) Tomatoes, skinned and chopped	64
Salt and pepper	–
	1,723

Calories per portion: 431

Soak soya mince in the hot water for thirty minutes. Cook spinach in the water clinging to the leaves after the final rinse. When very soft, drain, squeeze out all excess moisture, chop and keep warm. Heat oil, gently fry the onions without browning for two minutes. Add all the remaining ingredients, except the walnuts. Cook for five minutes, stirring from time to time. Transfer to a casserole with the spinach and soya. Sprinkle nuts over, cover and bake at 400°F/200°C (Gas Mark 6) for thirty minutes or until vegetables are cooked through.

Chef's tips:
(1) If using thawed frozen spinach warm between plates over boiling water then proceed as above.
(2) For a change in texture use green cabbage, Chinese leaves or chard (beet leaves) in place of the spinach. A smaller quantity will be needed — spinach reduces considerably in the cooking.
(3) A layer of baked beans or potatoes mashed with a little soya milk, can be placed in the middle of the vegetables for a more substantial and nutritious repast. This will, of course, add more calories.

STUFFED PEPPERS WITH PEAS AND SOYA

(six portions)

	Calories
1½ lb (¾kg) Starchy end-of-season garden peas (see Tips)	480
1 oz (25g) Texturized soya mince	50
¼ pint (150ml) Hot water to hydrate the mince	–
Salt and pepper	–
2 teaspoonsful (10ml) Marmite or yeast extract	12
6 Green peppers, prepared for stuffing	approx 320
Sauce:	
1 fl oz (25ml) Oil	260
3 oz (75g) Onions, chopped	15
3 oz (75g) Celery, chopped	9
1 Clove garlic, chopped	2
1 lb (450g) Tomatoes, skinned and chopped	64
Bouquet garni	–
Sprig of dill or celery leaves	–
Pinch of cumin	–
Small pinch curry powder	1
	1,213

Calories per portion: 202

Soak soya mince in the hot water for thirty minutes. Meanwhile, cook the peas until soft. Strain and sieve. Blend peas with the soya and stir in the Marmite. Season. Prepare the peppers. Cut a slice from stem end, remove membranes and seeds. Stuff with the pea mixture. Place in a fireproof casserole. Make the sauce. Heat the oil, fry onions, gently, without browning for two minutes. Stir in remaining sauce ingredients. Season. Pour sauce over peppers, cover and cook in oven at 400°F/200°C (Gas Mark 6) for 35-40 minutes. Check occasionally to make sure sauce does not evaporate. If necessary, add water or stock made from hot water flavoured with yeast extract.

Chef's tips:
(1) Wheat germ, toasted sesame seed or chopped nuts can be added to the stuffing to further enrich the food value of the dish.
(2) Serve with rice, boiled potatoes or couscous.
(3) This is an economical way of using the last-of-the-season peas when they have gone past their best. However, canned processed peas, drained, can be used instead.
(4) Use very ripe, juicy tomatoes.

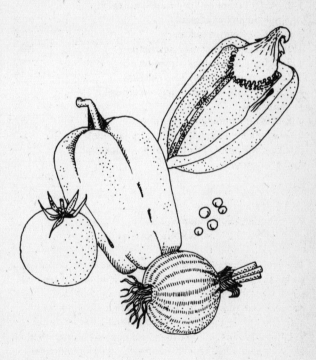

THREE-COLOUR PIE

(four large or six small portions)

	Calories
1 fl oz (25ml) Oil	260
1 lb (450g) Onions, sliced	80
1 teaspoonful (5ml) Curry powder	5
1 lb (450g) Tomatoes, skinned and chopped	64
½ lb (225g) Red peppers, seeded and chopped	80
1 teaspoonful (5ml) Paprika	–
3 Cloves garlic, chopped	6
1 lb (450g) Cooked (or frozen) spinach, drained and chopped	112
1 oz (25g) Peanut butter	175
¼ lb (100g) Wholemeal macaroni	380
1 oz (25g) Desiccated coconut	178
1 tablespoonful (15ml) Soy sauce	7
½ pint (275ml) Water (from macaroni, if possible)	–
¼ lb (100g) Pineapple, diced	52
1 teaspoonful (5ml) Cornflour } blended	20
5 tablespoonsful (75ml) Water } together	–
Salt and pepper	–
	1,419

Calories per portion: Large 355
Small 236

This is a layered pie where mixtures are placed on top of each other to give a colourful effect. Heat oil in a pan and sauté onions until soft and lightly browned for five minutes. Add curry powder and paprika. Cook thirty seconds. Stir in tomatoes, peppers and garlic. Simmer five minutes. Season with salt and pepper. Boil spinach in a little water until thawed or reheated for minimum time possible. Drain. Squeeze out excess water. Return to pan, add peanut butter and heat again. Season.

Meanwhile, cook macaroni in boiling, salted water for 20-25 minutes. Drain well, reserving liquid. Make the

sauce. Soak desiccated coconut in $\frac{1}{2}$ pint (275ml)
macaroni (or hot) water for twenty minutes. Liquidize.
Pour into a saucepan, heat, mix in blended cornflour,
bring to boil and cook, stirring, for two minutes. Remove
from heat, season and add soy sauce. Mix with the
macaroni. Place a layer of macaroni in bottom of a
fireproof dish. Cover with a layer of spinach and then with
a layer of tomato mixture. Repeat until all is used up,
ending with tomato mixture. Decorate top with diced
pineapple. Bake in oven preheated to 400°F/200°C (Gas
Mark 6) for fifteen to twenty minutes or until thoroughly
heated through. Serve immediately.

Chef's tips:
(1) Any egg-made pasta can be used for this dish.
(2) For a change use freshly made pancakes cut into thin
strips instead of macaroni.
(3) Spinach can be replaced by dark green cabbage.

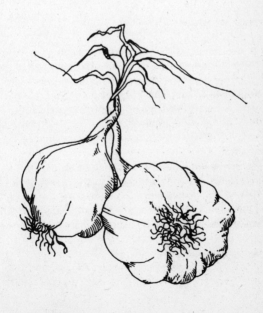

CHICK PEA PATTIES

(eight portions)

	Calories
1 lb (450g) Chick peas (cooked as in recipe on page 28, drained and cold)	1,280
1 tablespoonful (15ml) Chopped parsley and mint mixed together	–
1 oz (25g) Peanut butter	175
1 oz (25g) Desiccated coconut	178
1 Clove garlic, chopped	2
Juice of 1 lemon	4
Pinch each of cumin, mustard powder, cayenne or freshly ground black pepper	–
Salt	–
1 teaspoonful (5ml) Worcestershire sauce	2
1 oz (25g) Soya flour	120
1 tablespoonful (15ml) Oil	130
	1,891

Calories per portion: 236

Mash the drained chick peas thoroughly but not too finely (to the consistency of pease pudding). Blend with the other ingredients except soya flour and oil. Divide into 2 oz (50g) cakes. Coat lightly in soya flour. Grease a baking sheet with oil and bake cakes at 400°F/200°C (Gas Mark 6) for fifteen minutes.

Chef's tips:
(1) Serve the hot patties with a crisp salad, or, if your calorie allowance will permit, use to stuff warmed pitas to make delicious falafels.
(2) Cooked marrowfat, or starchy garden peas, or drained canned baked beans can be used for this recipe.

TOFU CHOP SUEY

(4 portions)

	Calories
2 fl oz (50ml) Oil	520
¼ lb (100g) Onions, chopped	20
1 Clove garlic, chopped	2
¼ oz (5g) Fresh peeled ginger, chopped	–
½ lb (225g) Celery, sliced	24
2 oz (50g) Peas	40
¼ lb (100g) Bean sprouts	12
1 tablespoonful (15ml) Soy sauce	7
Salt and pepper	–
¼ pint (150ml) Water	–
½ lb (225g) Amoy bean curd (tofu) cut into 1 in. (2.5cm) cubes	160
	785

Calories per portion: 196

First make a sauce. Heat half the oil in a pan and shallow fry the onions, covered with a lid, for about four minutes until softened but not browned. Add garlic, ginger and celery. Sauté four minutes then add peas and bean sprouts. Toss and stir in the water and soy sauce. Season to taste. Boil ten minutes. In a separate pan heat remaining oil and fry the tofu pieces, cut into cubes, until brown on both sides, turning once during the cooking. Serve the Tofu coated in the sauce.

Chef's tips:
(1) The Tofu can be moulded in a 1 inch (2.5cm) tray. In this way it is easier to cut into cubes.
(2) If using home-made tofu the calories will be slightly higher.

Note: Tofu can be purchased in any Oriental shop.

GENERAL

TWO-IN-ONE VEGETABLE HOT-POT

(four large or six small portions)

	Calories
2½ pints (1½ litres) Water	–
1 lb (450g) Small leeks	160
1 lb (450g) Celery, thinly sliced, if possible including root	48
1 lb (450g) Swedes, in chunks	80
1 lb (450g) Carrots, whole	80
1 lb (450g) Onions, whole	80
½ lb (225g) Peas	160
½ lb (225g) Cabbage, shredded	40
Bouquet garni	–
1 Clove garlic, chopped	2
2 tablespoonsful (30ml) Yeast extract	approx 60
1 lb (450g) Potatoes, quartered if large	400
1 oz (25g) Tomato paste	30
Salt and pepper	–
¼ pint (150ml) Skimmed milk (optional)	50
	1,190

Calories per portion: Large 297
                        Small 198

Trim leeks and tie in a bundle. Place carrots, celery, swedes and onions in a large stockpot or casserole, cover with the water, bring to the boil and cook, covered, for fifteen minutes. Add all remaining ingredients and cook for 20-30 minutes. Remove bouquet garni, adjust seasoning if necessary, untie the leeks. Strain off the vegetable stock, liquidize this with a little of the cooked vegetables (or sieve vegetables into the liquid) and if liked, add milk. Reheat. Serve as a starter soup. The vegetables form the main dish. Keep them warm while eating the first course.

Chef's Tips:
(1) This is a basic stock stew that can be adapted to use any vegetables in season. Soaked dried peas, beans and so on can be included.
(2) The vegetables can be served coated in a cheese or white sauce.
(3) Other vegetables can be added to the soup and it can be thickened with dried instant potato or with any thickening starch.
(4) If preferred the recipe can be cooked in the oven.
(5) When using extra ingredients keep a check on the total calories.

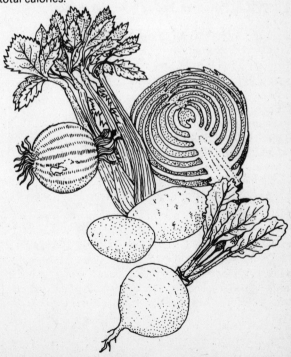

MIXED VEGETABLE AND NUT COULIBIAC

(six average or eight small portions)

	Calories
Batter:	
2 Eggs	180
¼ lb (100g) Wholemeal flour	376
¼ pint (150ml) Skimmed milk	50
¼ pint (150ml) Water	–
1 tablespoonful (15ml) Chopped parsley	–
Salt and pepper	–
1 fl oz (25ml) Oil	260
Filling:	
½ lb (225g) Peas, boiled until just tender	160
1 x 5 oz (150g) can Baked beans in tomato sauce	137
¼ lb (100g) Onions, chopped	20
¼ lb (100g) Potatoes, boiled until just tender, diced	100
2 teaspoonsful (10ml) Chopped coriander leaves or chervil	–
1 teaspoonful (5ml) Curry powder	5
½ oz (15g) Desiccated coconut	90
Sauce:	
2 Eggs, beaten	180
1 teaspoonful (5ml) Cornflour	20
¼ pint (150ml) Skimmed milk	50
¼ pint (150ml) Natural low-fat yogurt	80
1 teaspoonful (5ml) Desiccated coconut (for base of dish)	36
1 fl oz (25ml) Oil (for greasing dish etc.)	260
	————
	2,004

Calories per portion: Large 334
Small 250

Make a batter with the first four ingredients. Stir in parsley and seasoning. Cook 9-10 x 6 inch (15cm) pancakes in a little oil until all the batter is used. Spread pancakes on a tray to cool. Strain sauce from beans, (use sauce for a different recipe). Combine the beans with the rest of the ingredients for the filling. Make sauce. Mix cornflour to a smooth paste with a little of the milk. Heat remaining milk, add blended cornflour, bring to the boil and cook, stirring, for two minutes. Remove from heat. Cool a little and stir in the beaten eggs and yogurt. Add this to the vegetable mixture. Season. Brush a 2½ pint (1½ litre) pie dish with oil. Sprinkle desiccated coconut over the base. Line dish (base and sides) with pancakes, keeping two back for a lid. Fill dish with vegetable mixture. Top with reserved pancakes. Make sure all the pancakes are tucked in neatly and not overhanging sides of dish. Brush top with a little of the oil and bake at 350°F/180°C (Gas Mark 4) for 45 minutes. Turn out onto a warmed dish. Serve hot or cold.

Chef's tips:
(1) This is a useful way of using up left-over vegetables. They can be reheated mixed into the milky sauce and reheated in the pie to make an appetizing economical dish.
(2) Ring the changes with the vegetable mixture, and instead of spices use grated cheese.

HOT LENTILS AND CORN

(six portions)

	Calories
½ lb (225g) Lentils (soaked 2 hours)	680
½ lb (225g) Loose, fresh or frozen corn kernels	240
¼ lb (100g) Onions, chopped	20
Dressing:	
2 Eggs, hard-boiled, chopped	180
1 tablespoonful (15ml) Vinegar	–
¼ pint (150ml) Tangerine yogurt	125
1 teaspoonful (5ml) Honey	25
1 oz (25g) Cottage cheese	33
2 tablespoonsful (30ml) Water	–
Salt and pepper	–
Garnish:	
1 oz (25g) Chives, chopped	8
	1,311

Calories per portion: 219

Simmer soaked lentils in fresh water until tender, for an hour (approx). Drain. Shortly before end of lentil's cooking time, boil corn until just tender. Drain. Mix with lentils. Stir in chopped onion. Meanwhile sieve eggs and cottage cheese, stir in remaining dressing ingredients, add to lentils and, if necessary, reheat, gently stirring all the time. Transfer to a warmed serving bowl, garnish with the chives, and serve piping hot.

Chef's tips:
(1) When chives are unobtainable use the green part of salad onions; they are easy to 'chop' by snipping with sharp kitchen scissors.
(2) For those who find onions too pungent, raw leeks cut into thin rings make an excellent, milder substitute, (or chives).

OKRA AND WILD RICE

(four portions)

	Calories
¼ lb (100g) Wild rice (see method)	400
Boiling water (to cook rice)	–
1 fl oz (25ml) Oil	260
1 lb (450g) Okra, stems removed (take care not to break pods)	80
1 lb (450g) Tomatoes, skinned and chopped	64
½ lb (225g) Onions, chopped	40
1 Clove garlic, chopped	2
Bouquet garni	–
Salt and pepper	–
Pinch each of chilli pepper and oregano	–
¼ pint (150ml) Water (more if necessary)	–
	846

Calories per portion: 212

To prepare the rice wash through a strainer until water runs clear. Cover and soak overnight. Cover with three times its volume of boiling water, add salt, stir, cover and leave to simmer slowly for 30-45 minutes until all the water has been absorbed. Shallow fry onions in the oil until brown. Stir in tomatoes. Add okra and remaining ingredients. Bring to the boil, cover and simmer 20 minutes. Stir in cooked rice and serve piping hot.

Chef's tips:
(1) Extra cooked wild rice can be served separately.
(2) Always store this rice in a tightly covered container in a cool, dry place. It will keep indefinitely.
(3) Wild rice almost trebles in quantity when cooked.

BAKED STUFFED MARROW

(four portions)

	Calories
1 large or 2 small Marrows (3 lb (1¼kg) approx).	144
Stuffing:	
½ lb (225g) Mushrooms, chopped	16
7¾ oz (220g) can Baked beans in tomato sauce	213
2 Eggs, hard-boiled and chopped	180
2 oz (50g) Texturized soya mince	100
¼ pint (150ml) Hot water (to hydrate soya)	–
1 teaspoonful (5ml) Soy sauce	2
1 Clove garlic, chopped	2
Salt and pepper	–
1 teaspoonful (5ml) Curry powder	5
1 tablespoonful (15ml) Tomato paste	15
¼ lb (100g) Onions, chopped	20
¼ pint (150ml) Blackcurrant yogurt	125
Stock:	
½ pint (275ml) Water	–
Bouquet garni	–
Sprig fresh mint	–
3 oz (75g) Cheddar cheese, grated	360
	1,182

Calories per portion: 296

Trim ends from marrow. Cut into eight rings, if using large, or each of the small marrows into four rings. Remove all the seeds. Arrange pieces neatly in a large shallow dish. Make the filling. Mash beans in the tomato sauce, then add all the remaining filling ingredients and mix thoroughly. Fill marrow ring centres with this mixture, pressing it down until all is used up. Pour in the water, add the bouquet garni and mint. Cover with a lid or foil and bake at 375°F/190°C (Gas Mark 5) for 45 minutes to an hour, or until marrow is soft and filling cooked. Carefully remove marrow rings to a fireproof serving platter, sprinkle cheese over and brown quickly under a hot grill, or return to a hot oven for a few minutes. Strain pan juices, adjust seasoning and hand round separately.

Chef's tips:

(1) Vegetable marrows can be halved lengthwise, steamed until tender, or boiled until nearly cooked through. They can then be filled with a stuffing of your choice, the halves put together and tied, the marrow wrapped in foil or greaseproof paper and then put into a moderate oven for about thirty minutes until filling is cooked or heated through.

(2) Very large marrows can be a poor buy, as the texture may have gone coarse and there be an over-abundance of seeds. At this stage they are best for making preserves or wine!

(3) Fillings can include mashed chopped left-over root vegetables, cooked lentils, soya beans, etc.

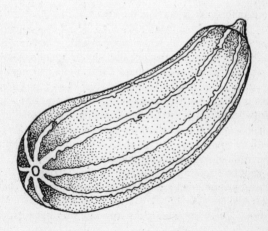

BRAISED LEEKS AU GRATIN

(four large or eight small portions)

	Calories
16 small or 8 large Leeks, trimmed	approx 288
8 thin slices Processed cheese, cut into thin strips	approx 840
4 Eggs, hard-boiled and sliced	360
Salt and pepper	–
¼ pint (150ml) Natural low-fat yogurt	80
1 level teaspoonful (5ml) Cornflour	20
3 tablespoonsful (45ml) Skimmed milk	15
1 tablespoonful (15ml) Chopped parsley or coriander leaves	–
2 oz (50g) Hazelnuts, chopped	360
	1,963

Calories per portion: Large 491
Small 245

Thoroughly wash leeks. Tie in bundles of four. Put in a
large pan, cover level with boiling water, add seasoning.
Cook for 12-15 minutes in an uncovered pan. When leeks
are tender, remove (reserve liquid), gently squeeze excess
moisture from the leeks, and lay them, green part neatly
tucked under, in a shallow fireproof dish. Keep the leeks
apart from each other. Cover with cheese strips and egg
slices. Put about ½ pint (275ml) leek liquid into a
saucepan and reheat to boiling point. Meanwhile blend
cornflour to a paste with the milk, stir into the yogurt and
then gradually stir into the boiling leek liquid. Reheat,
without boiling, for four minutes. Add the chopped
parsley, and seasoning to taste. Pour over the leeks. Bake
in a hot oven, 400°F/200°C (Gas Mark 6) for ten
minutes. Serve hot, garnished with the chopped nuts.

Chef's tips:
(1) Leeks can be very gritty. For this kind of recipe trim off any battered green parts. Cut away the root. Then insert the point of a sharp kitchen knife into the white part, cutting upwards towards the green leaves. Repeat in a criss-cross fashion. This will enable the inner leaves to be washed more thoroughly.
(2) The same kind of dish can be used with any of the following: french beans, courgettes, marrows, cauliflower, celery, fennel, asparagus, seakale, chicory or parsnips.

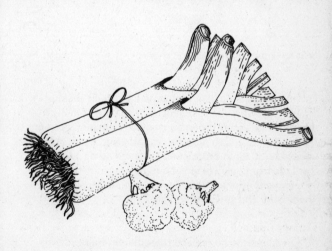

PEACH RICE PILAFF

(five portions)

	Calories
6 oz (175g) Brown rice	600
1 lb (450g) French or runner beans, trimmed and sliced	64
2 fl oz (50ml) Oil	520
2 oz (50g) Onions, chopped	10
1 teaspoonful (5ml) Curry powder	5
1 Clove garlic, chopped	2
1 tablespoonful (15ml) Tomato paste	15
Salt and pepper	–
1 lb (450g) Fresh peaches, stoned and sliced	160
$\frac{1}{4}$ pint (150ml) Tangerine yogurt	125
	1,501

Calories per portion: 300

Cook rice until soft and water absorbed, (for about 40-50 minutes). Cook beans in separate pan. Drain, reserve liquid. Mix with rice. In a saucepan heat oil, shallow fry onions until lightly browned, add curry powder, cook one minute, then add tomato paste, garlic and $\frac{1}{4}$ pint (150ml) bean liquid. Simmer, covered for ten minutes. Mix rice with this curry sauce and add remaining ingredients. Reheat gently, stirring constantly. Adjust seasoning if necessary and serve immediately.

Chef's tips:
(1) Peaches can be replaced by different fruits such as apricots, plums, pears, pineapple.
(2) Other types of rice can be used in place of brown rice if preferred. Wild rice, although a different plant all together, is very nutritious and can be used similarly.

Salads

RED, ORANGE AND WHITE SALAD

(one average or two small portions)

	Calories
¼ lb (100g) Cottage cheese with pineapple	126
1 Orange, peeled, pith removed, divided into segments	30
1 oz (25g) Green pepper, chopped	10
¼ lb (100g) Tomatoes, quartered	16
Salt and pepper	–
A little mustard and cress for garnish	–
	182

Calories per portion: average: 182
                      small: 91

Mix cottage cheese with green peppers and seasoning. Arrange in a bowl. Surround neatly with tomatoes and orange segments. Garnish with the cress.

Variation:
Curd cheese mixed with freshly chopped watercress could replace the cottage cheese with pineapple. To make this, chop ¼ bunch leaves and thin stalks of the cress, mix, with seasoning, into the curd cheese.

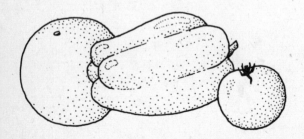

RUNNER BEAN MIX

(four portions)

	Calories
1 lb (450g) Runner beans, sliced, cooked and cold	64
2 Eggs, hard-boiled, cold, chopped	180
¼ lb (100g) New potatoes	100
¼ lb (100g) Cucumber, diced	12
2 Tomatoes, skinned, thinly sliced	16
1 teaspoonful (5ml) Chopped basil	–
1 teaspoonful (5ml) Chopped mint	–
½ lb (225g) Lettuce, shredded	24
¼ pint (150ml) Natural low-fat yogurt	80
Salt and pepper	–
1 Clove garlic, crushed	2
1 oz (25g) Apple chutney	45
2 oz (50g) Shelled peanuts	340
	863

Calories per portion: 216

Scrub new potatoes, boil until just tender. Meanwhile, mix garlic, seasoning and chutney into the yogurt. As soon as possible, dice the potatoes and toss in the yogurt mixture. Leave to cool. Using the beans as a centre, arrange the ingredients attractively either on one large serving platter or divided between four individual plates.

Chef's tips:
(1) Potato salads can be varied, but the secret of success is to mix the potatoes with the dressing of your choice while the vegetables are still warm and then leave to marinate.
(2) Any seasonal fresh herbs are excellent in salads. Use sparingly at first to see whether your family appreciates the flavour.

SALAD CRUNCH

(six portions)

	Calories
1½ lb (¾kg) Fresh spinach, shredded	120
2 oz (50g) Walnuts, chopped	310
½ lb (225g) Celery, chopped	24
½ oz (15g) Coriander leaves or parsley, chopped	–
½ lb (225g) Bean sprouts	24
Peanut Dressing:	
2 Eggs, hard-boiled, sliced	180
1 oz (25g) Peanut butter	175
¼ pint (150ml) Pineapple yogurt	130
2 oz (50g) Onions, grated	10
1 Clove garlic, chopped	2
Salt and pepper	–
Pinch curry powder	1
	——
	976

Calories per portion: 163

Before shredding the spinach, wash and dry carefully.
Combine first five ingredients. Make dressing. Sieve the
eggs into a small bowl. Mix in remaining ingredients.
Toss salad in dressing and serve immediately.

Chef's tips:
(1) Chopped young dandelion leaves or nasturtium leaves
or watercress can be added to the salad.

CHRISTMASTIDE SALAD

(four portions)

	Calories
1 lb (450g) Small, tight Brussels sprouts	160
½ lb (225g) Shelled chestnuts	400
½ lb (225g) Carrots, grated	40
¼ lb (100g) Curd cheese	160
Salt and pepper	–
	760

Calories per portion: 190

Cook sprouts until just tender, drain well. Cool. Prepare chestnuts (see tips), cook until tender, cool and chop. Mix sprouts with the chestnuts. Shortly before serving, grate the carrots, thoroughly blend into the cheese, season to taste and form into small balls. Mix into sprouts. Arrange in a serving bowl.

Chef's tips:
(1) Although more expensive, the small tight sprouts are always the best buy; cheaper loose-leaved samples can be wasteful and therefore dearer in the end.
(2) To prepare the chestnuts:
 1. Make a slit into the flat side of chestnuts, using the point of a small knife.
 2. Place chestnuts in a tray and bake at 425°F/220°C (Gas Mark 7) for eight minutes. The heat will crack the skin and open the nuts. Remove hard shell.
 3. Scald the chestnuts and peel the thin brown membrane.
 4. To cook, either roast chestnuts for twelve minutes at first stage or boil for twelve minutes at stage 3.

ITALIAN SALAD

(six portions)

	Calories
¾ lb (350g) Celery, thinly sliced	36
¼ lb (100g) Fennel, thinly sliced	12
¼ lb (100g) Processed cheese, cut into thin strips	420
¼ lb (100g) Cooked beetroot, cut into thin strips	60
2 oz (50g) Peeled chestnuts, halved or quartered	100
2 oz (50g) Walnuts, halved or quartered	310
¼ lb (100g) Carrots, grated	20
¼ lb (100g) Onions, chopped	20
Dressing:	
¼ pint (150ml) Apricot yogurt	130
Juice of 1 lemon	4
2 fl oz (50ml) Orange juice	24
Salt and pepper	–
1 teaspoonful (5ml) Wine vinegar	–
Garnish:	
4 Eggs, hard-boiled, sliced	360
12 Stuffed olives	84
	1,580

Calories per portion: 263

Mix salad ingredients. Whisk dressing ingredients to a cream, adding a little water if necessary. Toss salad in this mixture. Garnish with eggs and olives.

Chef's tips:
(1) Fennel has an aniseed taste to it which is very refreshing. However, if not liked, replace with bean sprouts or shredded cabbage or seakale or chicory.

COTTAGE CHEESE COLE SLAW

(four portions)

	Calories
1½ lb (¾kg) White cabbage, shredded	approx 120
¼ lb (100g) Onions, grated	20
¼ lb (100g) Celery, sliced	12
¼ lb (100g) Walnuts, roughly chopped	620
Dressing:	
¼ lb (100g) Cottage cheese	132
¼ lb (100g) Pineapple, finely chopped	52
Juice of 1 lemon	4
Salt and pepper	–
¼ teaspoonful Made mustard	4
½ teaspoonful Honey	13
1 Clove garlic, crushed	2
Garnish:	
1 Bunch watercress	16
	995

Calories per portion: 249

Combine first four ingredients. Make dressing. Mix all dressing ingredients together. Add to cabbage mixture and thoroughly blend. Serve garnished with watercress sprigs.

Chef's tips:
(1) Watercress sold in bunches with the grower's label attached should also carry a symbol guaranteeing it has been grown under stringent hygienic conditions.
(2) In place of celery use shredded chicory or cooked, diced celeriac.
(3) The cole slaw can be served on a bed of comfrey, lettuce or young spinach leaves.

NUTTY MACARONI PLATTER

(six average or eight small portions)

	Calories
½ lb (225g) Macaroni (short lengths)	816
¼ lb (100g) Celery, thinly sliced	12
¼ lb (100g) Walnuts, coarsley chopped	620
¼ lb (100g) Onions, finely chopped	20
Dressing:	
2½ fl oz (65ml) Slimmer's salad dressing	100
2½ fl oz (65ml) Natural low-fat yogurt	40
Juice of ½ lemon	2
1 teaspoonful (5ml) Made mustard	17
Salt and pepper	–
	1,627

Calories per portion: Large: 271
                    Small: 203

Cook macaroni until soft in boiling salted water. Drain. Transfer to a colander and rinse in cold water, drain very well. Make dressing. Mix salad dressing with yogurt, lemon juice, mustard and seasoning. Blend macaroni with celery, walnuts and onions, toss in the dressing. Serve chilled.

Chef's tips:
(1) Wholemeal macaroni or dried beans cooked and cold can be used in place of the macaroni.
(2) Although walnuts are suggested, any nuts are suitable; the commercially packed chopped mixed nuts would be ideal for those who like nuts that are very well chopped.
(3) Accompany the above salad with a mixed green salad, preferably including comfrey* and blanched young dandelion leaves and alfalfa (a lucerne rich in protein). Even clovers can be eaten in salad.

* Comfrey is a tall, rough-leaved ditch plant with clusters of whitish or purplish bells.

BEET AND SOYA CHIPLET SALAD

(four portions)

	Calories
¼ lb (100g) Dry soya chiplets, reconstituted (page 89)	approx 460
½ pint (275ml) Pineapple juice stock from cooking soya (page 89)	50
2 oz (50g) Cooked, cold corn kernels	60
¼ lb (100g) Potatoes, boiled, cold and sliced	100
6 oz (175g) Cooked, cold, beetroot, diced	90
2 oz (50g) Onions, chopped	10
1 Clove garlic, chopped	2
Juice and grated rind of 1 orange	30
Salt and pepper	–
¼ lb (100g) Tomatoes, sliced or chopped	16
Garnish:	
Green salad, including, if possible, young dandelion leaves, young nasturtium leaves and watercress	approx 40
	858

Calories per portion: 215

Combine all ingredients (except garnish), mix well, cover. Leave in a cool place for at least 1 hour for flavours to blend. Serve accompanied by the salad.

Chef's tips:
(1) Sprinkle chopped coriander, chervil, tarragon or celery leaves over for extra flavour.
(2) Replace corn kernels with cooked peas and add a little chopped mint to the mixture.

PANACHE SALAD

(six portions)

	Calories
¼ lb (100g) Haricot beans (soaked overnight)	300
1½ lb (¾kg) French beans, trimmed	96
2 oz (50g) Onions, chopped	10
1 Clove garlic, chopped	2
Salt and pepper	–
Dressing:	
2 Eggs, hard-boiled, sieved	180
2 oz (50g) Curd cheese	80
2 oz (50g) Chopped walnuts	310
2 fl oz (50ml) White vinegar	–
2 fl oz (50ml) Warm water	–
Garnish:	
2 tablespoonsful (30ml) Chopped parsley	–
	978

Calories per portion: 163

Cook the haricot beans until tender. Drain. Cook french
beans until tender. Drain. Mix the beans together while
still hot. Add onion, garlic and seasoning. Make dressing.
Mix cheese with vinegar and water, stir in the sieved eggs
and then the nuts. A little extra warm water (or warm
milk) can be added if mixture is too firm. Season. Stir
dressing into hot vegetables and serve immediately
garnished with chopped parsley.

Chef's tips:
(1) Any variety of dried bean can be used for this recipe
and any type of green bean (sliced if very large). Always
mix cold dressing into the hot mixture and allow flavours
to blend.
(2) A little fresh tarragon, chopped finely, can be added
(or any herbs you like, such as coriander leaves, lemon
balm, mint) to give a subtle change of flavour.

Snacks

WITHOUT CHEESE

STUFFED PANCAKES

(four portions)

	Calories
1 Egg, beaten	90
¼ pint (150ml) Skimmed milk	50
1 oz (25g) Wholemeal flour	95
1 oz (25g) White flour	100
Salt and pepper	–
Filling:	
1 small can Baked Beans in tomato sauce	137
1 oz (25g) Walnuts, chopped	155
1 oz (25g) Soya mince	50
1 fl oz (25ml) Oil	260
	937

Calories per portion: 234

Strain baked beans. Gently heat the sauce making up to
3 fl oz (75ml) with water if necessary, and pour over soya
mince. Return to pan, simmer over low heat for twenty
minutes. Meanwhile, make pancake batter with the egg,
milk, flours and seasoning. Using a little of the oil, fry four
large pancakes. Mix the soya mince mixture with the
beans and walnuts. (Add a little cayenne pepper or red
pepper sauce if liked) and use to fill each pancake. Roll
up, brush with oil and lay in a fireproof dish. Reheat in a
hot oven, 400°F/200°C (Gas Mark 6) for six to eight
minutes.

Variation:
The tomato sauce can be made spicy with the addition of
chopped garlic and a red chilli.

AVOCADO AND PEANUT DIP
(Served with soya strips and raw vegetables)

(six portions)

	Calories
Dip:	
1 lb (450g) Ripe avocado flesh (from 2-3 pears)	400
2 oz (50g) Onions, chopped	10
1 Clove garlic, chopped	2
2 oz (50g) Peanut butter	350
2 oz (50g) Freshly cooked and hot potatoes, mashed	50
Juice of 1 lemon	4
Salt and pepper	—
Vegetable garnish:	
½ lb (225g) Carrots, cut into sticks	40
¼ lb (100g) Cauliflower sprigs	20
¼ lb (100g) Cucumber, cut into 'fingers'	12
½ lb (225g) Celery, cut into sticks	24
¼ lb (100g) Dry soya strips, reconstituted (see page 89)	approx 460
½ pint (275ml) Vegetable stock (see page 89)	18
	1,390

Calories per portion: 232

Prepare the soya strips in the vegetable stock, simmer and cool. Drain. Make the dip. Scoop flesh from avocado pears. Mash and blend with remaining Dip ingredients. Sieve or liquidize. (A little hot water can be added if required). Cool. Transfer to a serving bowl. Chill. Arrange vegetables on a serving platter, serve with the soya and Dip in separate bowls.

N.B. Soya strips can be served on cocktail sticks. They are cut, like beef for Beef Stroganoff in 1½ inch x ¼ inch (3.5cm x ½cm) pieces.

CURRIED SOYA CUTLETS

(eight cutlets)

	Calories
1 lb (450g) Mashed potatoes	400
2 oz (50g) Soya mince	100
1 fl oz (25ml) Oil	260
¼ lb (100g) Onions, chopped	20
1 teaspoonful (5ml) Curry powder	5
1 tablespoonful (15ml) Soy sauce	7
1 tablespoonful (15ml) Tomato paste	15
2 Cloves garlic, chopped	4
1 teaspoonful (5ml) Honey	25
2 Fresh mint leaves, chopped	–
¼ pint (150ml) Hot water	–
2 oz (50g) Fresh or frozen peas, cooked, roughly mashed	40
1 oz (25g) Fresh or frozen corn	30
1 Green chilli, sliced	1
Salt and pepper	–
2 oz (50g) Soya flour	240
	1,147

Calories per portion: 143

Sieve mashed potatoes. Heat oil and fry onions for two to three minutes until lightly browned. Stir in curry powder. Cook thirty seconds, then add tomato paste, soy sauce, garlic, mint, honey and seasoning. Dilute with the hot water. Boil five minutes and pour over the soya mince. Leave to soak for thirty minutes. Cool. When completely cold, blend in the potatoes, peas, chilli and corn. Season. Divide into eight and shape into cutlets. Coat with soya flour. Place on foiled baking sheet and bake for fifteen minutes at 400°F/200°C (Gas Mark 6). Serve hot or cold.

Variations:
Reduce mashed potato by half and replace with same amount of cooked semolina or corn meal. When making semolina, use 2 oz (50g) per ½ pint (275ml) water to make a very thick porridge.

Another alternative is to blend mashed peas or beans into potatoes.

Soya mince can be replaced by ground almonds.

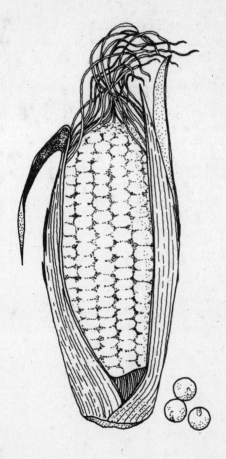

OVEN-ROASTED SOYA BEANS

	Calories
1 lb (450g) Soya beans	600
½ oz (15g) Salt	–

Soak beans overnight. Boil for 1-1½ hours in salted water until just tender. Drain thoroughly. Spread out in a roasting tray and bake at 350°F/180°C (Gas Mark 4) for thirty minutes or until brown. Sprinkle with salt while still warm. Serve cold.

Uses:
(1) Soya beans prepared in this way are delicious for pre-meal 'nibbles' or for parties.
(2) Give children oven-roasted soya beans rather than sweets.
(3) Ground, roasted soya beans can be blended to porridge or mixed in any other cereal.
(4) Try ground, roasted beans liquidized with a vegetable purée for a soup or sauce.

WITH CHEESE

EGGS WITH SPROUT CREAM

(four portions)

	Calories
4 Eggs, hard-boiled and hot	360
2¼ lb (1kg) Brussels sprouts, trimmed	360
1 oz (25g) Onion, sliced	5
½ oz (15g) Butter	113
Salt and pepper	–
3 tablespoonsful (45ml) Skimmed milk	15
2 oz (50ml) Cheshire cheese, grated	220
Paprika pepper	–
	1,073

Calories per portion: 268

Cook the sprouts and onion in boiling salted water until very tender. Drain. Liquidize with the skimmed milk. Stir in the butter and season to taste. Lay eggs in a shallow fireproof dish. Cover with the sprout cream, spread the cheese over and brown under a hot grill. Sprinkle with paprika.

Variations:
Any green vegetable could be used for the coating, spring greens, spinach, cabbage, or, for a colour and flavour contrast, red cabbage cooked with a few caraway seeds. If calories and taste permit, in place of the skimmed milk use cream or yogurt.

APPLE 'N' CHEESE CRISPBREAD

(one portion)

	Calories
1½ oz (40g) Cheddar cheese, grated	180
Pinch each of salt and cayenne	–
¼ teaspoonful Made mustard	4
1 tablespoonful (15ml) Skimmed milk	5
½ Eating apple, peeled, cored, thinly sliced	20
2 Starch reduced crispbreads	36
Parsley sprigs for garnish	–
	245

Mix cheese, seasonings, mustard and milk together,
whisk with a fork. Lay apple slices on the crispbread,
cover with cheese mixture. Cook under a hot grill until
brown on top. Serve immediately, garnished with parsley.

Variations:
Other kinds of hard cheese can be used for this recipe. In
place of sliced apple, spread the crispbreads with chutney
or chopped onion and then cover with the cheese, or
when in season, replace apple with peaches or apricots.

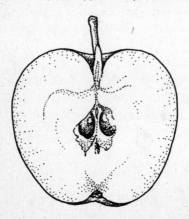

SAVOURY STUFFED APPLES

(four portions)

	Calories
4 largish Cooking apples	approx 280
3 oz (75g) Cheddar cheese, grated	360
2 oz (50g) Seedless raisins	140
1 teaspoonful (5ml) Grated onion	1
	781

Calories per portion: 196

Cut round the circumference of the apple, skin deep, no more, to score the peel. Core and stand apples in a shallow fireproof dish. Pour a little cold water round. Mix remaining ingredients and fill core cavities. Cook in oven at 375°F/190°C (Gas Mark 5) for about 45 minutes, or until fruit is tender.

Variations:
Replace cheese with the same amount of any ground nuts, or with chopped hard-boiled egg, or with a mixture of egg and cheese.

As a change from raisins try minced dates.

STUFFED PRUNES

(four portions)

	Calories
16 Dried prunes	160
2 oz (50g) Curd cheese	80
½ teaspoonful Marmite	3
¼ lb (100g) Chicory leaves	approx 12
	255

Calories per portion: 64

Soak prunes overnight. Drain. If necessary stone the fruit.
Mix curd cheese with Marmite, moistening with a little
skimmed milk if needed. Use mixture to stuff prunes.
Serve on a bed of chicory leaves.

Variations:
Instead of prunes use dried peaches or apricots. Soak and
cook these fruit slightly then cool and drain.

Desserts

SPICED APPLE BREAD PUDDING

(four average or six small portions)

	Calories
¼ lb (100g) Wholemeal bread, cut into small dice	260
2½ fl oz (65ml) Pineapple juice (or orange juice)	30
Pinch each of cinnamon, ground cloves, ginger	–
1 Egg, beaten	90
1 oz (25g) Honey	82
½ lb (225g) Cheap eating apples, peeled, cored, sliced	80
1 oz (25g) Seedless raisins	70
1 oz (25g) Peanut butter, melted	175
2 tablespoonsful (30ml) Cold water	–
	787

Calories per portion: Average 197
　　　　　　　　　　　　Small 131

Put diced bread in a bowl. Combine water, egg, spices, honey and pineapple juice, pour over bread. Leave to soak fifteen to thirty minutes. Place a layer of bread mixture in base of a shallow fireproof dish, cover with a layer of apples, sprinkle a few raisins over, continue to layer, ending with bread, until all the mixture is used. Spread peanut butter over and bake in preheated oven at 350°F/180°C (Gas Mark 4) for about 45 minutes until cooked through. Serve hot. Accompany with cold yogurt if liked.

Variations:
The bread can be used as crumbs if preferred. In place of apples try stoned, chopped plums. We recommend using ripe fruit as this requires less extra sweetening.

PEAR AND GOOSEBERRY CRUMBLE

(four large or six small portions)

	Calories
2 x ¼ lb (100g) Ripe pears, peeled, cored and sliced	80
½ lb (225g) Hard green gooseberries, topped and tailed	40
1 oz (25g) Honey	82
¼ Jamaica ginger cake, crumbed	approx 580
	782

Calories per portion: Average 196
Small 130

Mix fruit together and lay in base of a shallow fireproof dish. Dribble the honey over. Spread cake crumbs on top. Bake for 30-35 minutes at 350°F/180°C (Gas Mark 4). Cover with foil during baking to keep the crumbs moist. Remove foil for last ten minutes cooking time. Serve on its own, or with blackcurrant yogurt or with custard made with skimmed milk.

Variation:
Any seasonal fruits, or mixtures of fruits are suitable for this recipe.

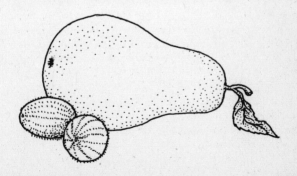

ORANGE OR WINE CUSTARD CREAM

(four portions)

	Calories
2 oz (50g) Honey	164
1 Egg	90
4 Egg yolks	260
¼ pint (150ml) Orange juice	60
or	
Sweet wine (125 calories)	
1 drop each Rose water and orange essence	–
	574

Calories per portion: With orange juice 144
    With wine 160

Place egg, yolks, orange juice or wine and honey in a thick, preferably metal, bowl and with an electric whisk, beat for five minutes. Then put bowl over a pan of boiling water and cook, like a custard, still whisking for about five minutes, until thick and foamy. Remove from heat. Whisk again for three minutes, add essences. Serve hot on its own or with stewed fruit.

Variations:
Leave custard to cool and serve either on its own or with a fresh fruit salad.

ALMOND AND CARROT BLANCMANGE

(four average or six small portions)

	Calories
¼ lb (100g) Flaked almonds	680
½ pint (275ml) Hot water	–
1 oz (25g) Honey	82
½ oz (15g) Gelatine	35
½ lb (225g) Young carrots, grated	40
5 fl oz (150ml) Cold water (to dissolve gelatine)	–
1 small Slice fresh ginger, chopped	–
2 drops each Rose and Orange Flower essence	–
	837

Calories per portion: Average 209
                       Small 139

Liquidize almonds, hot water, honey. Dissolve gelatine in the cold water (to do this, put water in a cup, sprinkle gelatine in and stir. Place cup in a pan of hot water over low gas, and heat, stirring, without the outside water boiling, until gelatine has dissolved and is clear). Cool slightly, add to almond mixture. Cool. Stir in ginger, carrots and essences. Pour into a mould and leave to set. Serve on its own or accompanied by a little fresh fruit salad.

Variation:
The carrots can be boiled in ¼ pint (150ml) water, with the ginger and 1 oz (25g) honey until soft and the liquid has all evaporated, cooled and then added, with the essence to the almond mixture. This gives a sweeter, softer texture. With the additional honey add another 82 calories to the overall total.

SOYA SWEETMEAT ORIENTAL

(36-38 small balls)

	Calories
$\frac{1}{4}$ pint (150ml) Pineapple juice	60
2 oz (50g) Unflavoured soya mince	100
2 oz (50g) Walnuts	310
2 oz (50g) Peanut butter	350
1 oz (25g) Honey	82
2 oz (50g) Desiccated coconut	356
$\frac{1}{4}$ lb (100g) Dried dates, finely chopped	240
Pinch mixed spice	–
$\frac{1}{2}$ oz (15g) Cocoa powder, sieved	64
2 drops Vanilla essence	–
1 drop Rose water essence	–
1 drop Almond essence	–
	1,562

Calories per ball: approximately 43

Bring pineapple juice to near boiling point. Pour over soya mince, leave to soak for thirty minutes. Then add all other ingredients except cocoa and essences. Transfer to a thick-based saucepan, heat gently and cook for ten minutes, stirring. Remove from heat, add essences and leave to cool. When cold divide mixture into small balls. Coat in cocoa powder. Serve with coffee.

GRANDMA'S DELIGHT

(four portions)

	Calories
3 medium Oranges, peeled, all pith removed	90
½ pint (275ml) Water	–
Liquid sweetener to taste	–
1 fl oz (25ml) Grand Marnier (or to taste)	93
	183

Calories per portion: 46

Cut the oranges into rings. Divide between individual bowls, cover and keep cool. Put roughly sliced peel of two oranges in a pan with the water, bring to the boil, cover, simmer five minutes, strain, add the sweetener, then the liqueur. Cool. Pour liquid over orange rings and serve.

Variations:
Boil the peel in less water, strain, sweeten. When cold mix into an orange yogurt and spoon over orange rings. Grapefruits, tangerines, etc., can be used in place of oranges.

BAKED BANANA AND PEAR TOPPER

(six portions)

	Calories
2 small Ripe bananas, peeled and sliced	130
½ lb (225g) Ripe pears, peeled and sliced	80
Pinch nutmeg or cinnamon	–
1 oz (25g) Chocolate sponge cake crumbs	116
2 Eggs, beaten until frothy	180
½ pint (275ml) Skimmed milk	100
2 teaspoonsful (10ml) Soft brown sugar (or liquid sweetener)	46
1 teaspoonful (5ml) Cocoa powder, sieved	22
2 drops Vanilla essence ⎫	–
1 drop Almond essence ⎬ measure with a dropper	–
1 drop Orange essence ⎭	–
	674

Calories per portion: 112

Mix fruit with cake crumbs and spices. Divide between six ramekins or small fireproof dishes. Mix beaten eggs with milk, sugar, cocoa, essences to make a custard. Pour over fruit mixture. Place dishes in a deep tray half filled with hot but not boiling water. Bake in bottom section of preheated oven at 350°F/180°C (Gas Mark 4) for 25-35 minutes or until set. Serve hot or cold.

Variations:
Mix bananas with a blackcurrant purée made by simmering the currants in a little sweetened water until the fruit is soft and nearly all the juice evaporated, sieve, cool.

Refreshing Drinks

TOMATO CUP

(three-four drinks)

	Calories
½ pint (275ml) Tomato juice	60
½ pint (275ml) Natural low-fat yogurt	160
	220

Calories per drink: Large 74
Small 55

Mix ingredients, shake thoroughly. Serve chilled.

TOMATO COCKTAIL

(three-four drinks)

	Calories
1¾ pints (1 litre) Tomato juice	210
3 fl oz (75ml) Orange juice	36
½ level teaspoonful Salt	–
Juice of ¼ lemon	1
Dash Worcestershire sauce	–
2 teaspoonsful (10ml) Sugar	46
	293

Calories per drink: Large 98
Small 73

Mix ingredients. Serve chilled.

CITRUS BOOSTER

(one drink)

	Calories
$\frac{1}{4}$ pint (150ml) Orange juice	60
Juice of 1 lemon	4
1 Egg yolk	65
1 teaspoonful (5ml) Honey	25
	154

Mix thoroughly, shake. Serve at room temperature.

N.B. This is very refreshing if you are feeling tired. A dash of sherry can be added if liked.

OLD-FASHIONED EGG-NOGG

(one drink)

	Calories
1 Egg, separated	90
1 teaspoonful (5ml) Honey	25
$\frac{1}{4}$ pint (150ml) Milk	93
Pinch each of ginger and nutmeg	–
1 tablespoonful (15ml) Rum	30
	238

Whisk egg white until stiff, then beat in the honey. In a separate bowl beat remaining ingredients. Fold in egg white. Pour into a tall glass and serve at room temperature.

N.B. This can be appreciated when you do not fancy a 'proper' meal. Ideal when spring-cleaning or decorating etc!

EYE-OPENER

(one large or two small drinks)

	Calories
¼ pint (150ml) Apricot yogurt	140
¼ pint (150ml) Skimmed milk	50
1 teaspoonful (5ml) Honey	25
	215

Calories per drink: Large 215
　　　　　　　　　　　Small 108

Mix ingredients thoroughly. Chill.

N.B. This is a refreshing morning drink that is also useful when accompanied by fruit as a 'quickie' breakfast.

HONOLULU

(one large or two small drinks)

	Calories
¼ pint (150ml) Pineapple juice, unsweetened	60
2 Egg whites	50
¼ pint (150ml) Soda water	–
2 Ice cubes	–
Mint leaves for garnish	–
	110

Calories per drink: Large 110
　　　　　　　　　　　Small 55

Place first four ingredients in a cocktail shaker and mix well. Serve garnished with mint leaves.

ICED TEA FLIP

(one large or two small drinks)

	Calories
½ pint (275ml) Green tea	4
2 Egg yolks	130
1 drop Vanilla essence	–
2 Ice cubes	–
2 Mint leaves	–
	134

Calories per drink: Large 134
Small 67

As soon as the tea is made add the mint leaves and brew
for six minutes. Strain. Cool. Thoroughly mix with the
other ingredients, preferably in a cocktail shaker.

N.B. This is a good drink when feeling jaded.

CIDER VINEGAR SPECIAL

(one drink)

	Calories
2 teaspoonsful (10ml) Honey	50
1 tablespoonful (15ml) Cider vinegar	1
½ pint (275ml) Water	–
	51

Heat a little of the water, pour over honey in a glass.
When the honey has dissolved add remaining water and
stir in the vinegar. Drink hot or cold.

CARROT AND RHUBARB QUENCHER

(four drinks)

	Calories
¼ lb (100g) Rhubarb, trimmed and diced	8
1 pint (550ml) Water	–
½ oz (15g) Honey	41
¼ lb (100g) Carrots, thinly sliced	20
1 small slice Fresh ginger	–
	69

Calories per drink: 17

Cook rhubarb with honey and half the water until very soft. Cool. Liquidize with the remaining ingredients. Serve icy cold, neat or diluted with soda water.

JAMAICAN QUAFF

(two large or four small drinks)

	Calories
2 oz (50g) Desiccated coconut	356
1 pint (550ml) Water	–
1 fl oz (25ml) Lime juice cordial	30
	386

Calories per drink: Large 193
                         Small 97

Put coconut and water in a saucepan bring to boil, cover and simmer for five minutes. Cool. Liquidize. Stir in cordial. Serve chilled with ice cubes, if liked.

Miscellaneous

ALL SEASON'S PÂTÉ

(eight portions)

	Calories
$\frac{1}{2}$ lb (225g) Spinach, coarsely chopped	40
$\frac{1}{2}$ lb (225g) Cabbage (spring) greens, coarsely chopped	24
$\frac{1}{4}$ lb (100g) Brussels sprouts, finely shredded	40
$\frac{1}{4}$ lb (100g) Onions, finely chopped	20
2 Cloves garlic, crushed	4
5 Fresh mint leaves, finely chopped	–
1 lb (450g) Leeks, well trimmed, thinly sliced	160
1 tablespoonful (15ml) Chopped parsley	–
4 Eggs, beaten	360
$\frac{1}{4}$ pint (150ml) Natural low-fat yogurt	80
$\frac{1}{4}$ lb (100g) Cottage cheese, sieved	132
$\frac{1}{2}$ lb (225g) Ripe avocado pear flesh	200
1 teaspoonful (5ml) Honey	25
Salt and freshly ground black pepper	–
1 oz (25g) Powdered gelatine	70
4 fl oz (100ml) Water (to dissolve gelatine)	–
	1,155

Calories per portion: 144

Boil the vegetables and herbs in salted water for five minutes. Drain. Place in a cloth and squeeze out any water left clinging to the leaves after cooking. Pour beaten eggs in a large bowl, add cottage cheese, yogurt, seasoning and honey, then add the avocado pulp. Meanwhile, dissolve gelatine in the water, (see page 73), cool, stir into the egg mixture and beat in the vegetables. Transfer to 8 x $\frac{1}{2}$ pint (275ml) fireproof dishes. Arrange these in baking trays half filled with hot, but not boiling, water and bake at 350°F/180°C (Gas Mark 4) for an hour or until set. Cool.

Chef's tips:
(1) This pâté is light, flavoursome and rich in the nutrients needed for a light meal. Accompany with a large salad and granary bread or use as a starter with fingers of wholemeal toast.
(2) For a change, omit cabbage greens or Brussels sprouts and replace with ½ lb (225g) finely chopped mushrooms. Add mushrooms with the avocado pear to the eggs and proceed as above.

HOT CUCUMBER SOUP

(six average or eight small portions)

	Calories
1 lb (450g) Cucumber, halved lengthwise, seeded and diced	approx 48
¼ lb (100g) Carrots, diced	20
2 oz (50g) Onion, chopped	20
2 oz (50g) Fresh or frozen peas	40
2½ pints (1½ litres) Water (or white stock)	–
1½ fl oz (40ml) Vegetable oil	390
1½ oz (40g) Wholemeal flour	141
Salt and pepper	–
Pinch nutmeg	–
2½ fl oz (65ml) Natural low-fat yogurt	40
	699

Calories per portion: Large 116
Small 87

Bring water to the boil, add cucumber, carrots and onions. Cover and simmer for fifteen minutes. Add peas and cook for a further fifteen minutes or until the vegetables are tender. Strain, reserving liquid and vegetables. Heat oil in a clean saucepan, stir in the flour, cook for two minutes until a sandy texture is reached. Gradually add the soup liquid, bring to boil, cook three minutes. Add vegetables, seasoning, nutmeg and yogurt. Reheat but do not boil. Serve piping hot.

Variations:
Runner or french beans can be added in place of peas; if calories and taste permit, the yogurt can be replaced by either milk or single cream.

A little fresh mint leaf or lemon-grass herb, or grated lemon rind will enhance the flavour.

SOYA MILK FROM SOYA FLOUR

(yields two pints approximately)

	Calories
½ lb (225g) Soya flour	960
2 pints (1¼ litres) Water	–
½ oz (15g) Honey	41
A little salt	–
	1,001

Calories per pint: 500

Gradually stir the water into the flour, taking care the mixture is not lumpy. Leave to stand for two hours. Cook in double boiler for twenty minutes. Strain through muslin or cheese cloth and sweeten with the honey. Add a little salt. Cool. Store in sterilized jars or bottles, cover securely and keep in a cold place. If stored at 40°F (4.5°C) or just below, it will keep for at least a week.

N.B. Soya milk, which can be frozen in sealed containers, can be used in recipes requiring ordinary milk.

HOME-MADE TOFU CHEESE

(also called Bean Curd)

(Yield approximately 12 oz-1 lb (350g-450g))

	Calories
2 pints (1¼ litres) Soya milk (page 87)	1,000
¼ teaspoonful Tartaric acid	–
2 tablespoonsful (30ml) Hot water	–
¾ oz (20g) Salt	–
1 teaspoonful (5ml) Soy sauce	2
or	
Pinch of monosodium glutamate	–
	1,002

Calories per oz (25g) – allowing for liquid loss in the preparation approximately: 56-73

Bring milk to the boil. Cool to blood heat, 98.4°F (37°C). Dissolve tartaric acid in the hot water, add to the milk. Leave to stand twenty minutes until it thickens and forms into curds. Cut with a knife into chunks. Transfer to a saucepan, add salt and soy sauce, bring to the boil, stirring constantly to prevent danger of scorching. Strain through muslin or cheese cloth. Transfer the curds that remain in the cloth to a shallow tray, an inch (2.5cm) deep. Cut into cubes and leave to get cold. The Tofu is then ready to be used for recipes.

Chef's tips:
(1) This cheese is perishable and should be used up quickly or packed in polythene bags and deep-frozen. Storage life is three months in a freezer.
(2) The curd can be sweetened lightly with a little sugar, glucose or honey.

RECONSTITUTED SOYA CHIPLETS

(1)
1 pint (550ml) Water
1 oz (25g) Marmite (or yeast extract)
Salt and pepper
2 Cloves garlic, chopped
$\frac{1}{4}$ pint (150ml) Pineapple juice
1 teaspoonful (5ml) Oil
$\frac{1}{4}$ lb (100g) Dry soya chiplets
3 tablespoonsful (45ml) Vinegar

Heat water, add Marmite and dissolve. Stir in seasoning, garlic, vinegar and pineapple juice. Bring to boil, cover, simmer for three to four minutes. Cool for four minutes* then add soya pieces. Leave to soak for 35 minutes. Reheat and simmer gently for 15-25 minutes without allowing to boil. Leave to cool. When cold add the oil. Drain well. The soya chiplets are now ready to serve with raw or cooked vegetables. The stock (approx. 100 calories per pint (550ml)) can be used for sauces, soups, etc. A little can be added to salads as a simple dressing.

(2)
$\frac{1}{4}$ lb (100g) Dry soya chiplets
Vegetable stock:
2 oz (50g) Onions, chopped
2 oz (50g) Celery, chopped
2 oz (50g) Carrots, chopped
1 tablespoonful (15ml) Marmite (or yeast extract)
$\frac{3}{4}$ pint (425ml) Water
Bouquet garni
Salt and pepper

Bring vegetables to the boil in the water, add Marmite, seasoning and bouquet garni, cover and simmer for twenty minutes. Strain. Cool for four minutes then, using $\frac{1}{2}$ pint (275ml) of the liquid, proceed as above from * mark. The stock in this method is approximately 18 calories per $\frac{1}{2}$ pint (275ml).
N.B. Dry soya chiplets are fortified with additional nutrients. They are approximately 460 calories per $\frac{1}{4}$ lb (100g).

HOME-MADE CHEESE BISCUITS (WITH SALAD)

(twenty-four biscuits approximately)

	Calories
2 oz (50g) Wholemeal flour	188
Pinch each celery salt and garlic salt	–
½ oz (15g) Butter	113
¼ lb (100g) Cheddar cheese, grated	480
Cold water to mix	–
1 oz (25g) Flour (for rolling out)	94
⅓ oz (10g) Butter (for greasing baking sheet)	75
	950

Calories per biscuit: approx 39

Stir salts into flour. Rub in butter and add the cheese. Mix and bind with about a tablespoonful (15ml) cold water, to make a firm dough. Roll out to about ⅛ inch (.313 cm) thick. Cut into rounds and place on a lightly greased baking sheet. Prick each biscuit with a fork. Bake in a hot oven, 450°F/230°C (Gas Mark 8) for five to eight minutes until golden brown. Leave on tray for a few minutes to firm before cooling on a rack. Serve with a mixed salad.

Variations:
Replace half the wholemeal flour with an equal quantity of soya flour. For a nutty texture add sesame seeds to the mixture with the cheese.

Suggested Menus

Without being allowed a little luxury dieting can become a bore. This is why in the menus listed below an allowance is made each day for you to have at least one special treat; a cup of tea with milk and honey perhaps, or a home-made biscuit, a glass of wine or a quaff of home-made beer, or maybe extra vegetables. Four menus are for 1,000 calories per day and three for 1,500 calories. On this diet weight loss is consistent but not rapid. There is no feeling of being a martyr to a cause but real satisfaction in seeing the inches disappearing. Some of the dishes contain eggs, milk or cheese. However for those who do not eat dairy foods or eggs there are alternative dishes contained in the book.

Day 1 :— (Allowance 1,000 calories)

Breakfast	Calories
Nutty Bites menu (page 21)	216
1 cup mint tea	–
Lunch	
All Season's Pâté (page 84)	144
Small green salad	10
2 starch reduced crispbreads	38
1 small banana	65
2 cups black coffee	4
Dinner	
$\frac{1}{2}$ grapefruit	15
Chick Pea and Vegetable Casserole (page 28)	250
2 tablespoonsful boiled chopped spinach	approx 14
2 Soya Sweetmeats (page 74)	86
1 cup black coffee	2
	———
	844

Day 2:— (Allowance 1,000 calories)
Breakfast

	Calories
Sesame Spread Menu (page 25)	287
1 cup lemon tea	2

Lunch

Eggs with Sprout Cream (page 65)	268
2 cups black coffee	4

Dinner

Hot Cucumber Soup, small portion (page 86)	87
Nutty Macaroni Platter, small portion (page 56)	203
2 oz (50g) strawberries	10
1 cup black coffee	2
	———
	863

Day 3:— (Allowance 1,000 calories)
Breakfast

	Calories
2 oz (50g) cold stewed apple (with liquid sweetener) served with	20
1 oz (25g) cornflakes	100
1 cup lemon tea	2

Lunch

3 oz (75g) cottage cheese	99
Large mixed salad	25
1 slice wholemeal bread and butter	121
1 cup black coffee	2

Dinner

$\frac{1}{4}$ pint (150ml) tomato juice	30
Mixed Vegetable and Nut Coulibiac, large portion (page 40)	334
Baked Banana and Pear Topper (page 76)	112
2 cups black coffee	4
	———
	849

Day 4:— (Allowance 1,000 calories)

Breakfast	Calories
¼ pint (150ml) orange juice	60
1 boiled egg	90
2 Rye crispbreads (starch reduced)	38
¼ oz (5g) butter	57
1 cup lemon tea	2

Lunch	
Stuffed Pancakes (page 60)	234
Small green salad	10
1 ripe pear	40
1 cup black coffee	2

Dinner	
Two-in-One Vegetable Hot-Pot, large portion (page 38)	297
2 small scoops lemon sorbet water ice	approx 60
1 cup black coffee	2
	892

Day 5:— (Allowance 1,500 calories)

Breakfast	Calories
Nutty Milk Compote menu (page 18)	348
1 cup lemon verbena tea	–

Lunch	
Avocado and Peanut Dip menu (page 61)	232
1 slice rye bread	67

Dinner	
¼ lb (144g) slice Honeydew melon	20
¼ pint (150ml) dry wine	100
Baked Stuffed Marrow (page 44)	296
Wine Custard Cream (page 72)	160
	1,223

Day 6:— (Allowance 1,500 calories)
Breakfast   Calories
Wholemeal Pancake menu (page 23)   221
2 cups lemon tea   4
Lunch
Italian Salad (page 54)   263
1 slice granary bread   67
1 ripe apple   40
2 cups black coffee   4
Teatime
2 cups lemon tea   4
2 digestive wheatmeal biscuits   140
Dinner
½ x 10 oz. (283g) can cream of celery soup   73
Peach Rice Pilaff (page 48)   300
¼ pint (150g) dry wine   100
Almond and Carrot Blancmange, small portion
    (page 73)   139
                                                                  ———
                                                                 1,355

Day 7:— (Allowance 1,500 calories)
Breakfast   Calories
½ grapefruit   15
Porridge Bee (page 20)   253
1 cup lemon tea   2
Lunch
Tomato Cocktail, small (page 78)   73
Runner Bean Mix (page 51)   216
1 slice granary bread   67
1 cup black coffee   2
Teatime
2 cups lemon tea   4
2 oatmeal cookie biscuits   80
Dinner
½ avocado pear and lemon juice   125
¼ pint (150ml) dry wine   100
Three-colour Pie, large portion (page 34)   355
Grandma's Delight (page 75)   46
1 cup black coffee   2
                                                                  ———
                                                                 1,340

Recipe Index